GET *OVER* IT

GET OVER IT

The Realest Guide to Stress Management

ANNA KATZ

DRIVEN

DRIVEN
Published in the United States by Driven, an imprint of Zeitgeist™,
a division of Penguin Random House LLC, New York.
penguinrandomhouse.com

ISBN: 978-0-593-67460-4

ONE+ONE

Produced by One+One Books
Written by Anna Katz
Book design by Carol Bobolts and Red Herring Design

Printed in the United States of America
1st Printing

Image credits: Shutterstock.com: A Aleksii (fruit) p. 44; Alyona Zhitnaya (X) pgs. 5, 11, 17, 23, 47, 49, 61, 65, 71, 85, 89, 91, 99, 105, 113, 114, 121; Artco (house, classroom) p. 44; BEMPhoto31 (DNA) p. 44; lanastance (redirect icon) pgs. 57, 60, 62, 66, 74, 76, 96, 98, 100, 104, 106, 108, 112, 115, 118, 120; matsabe (heart) p. 44; M-Vector (head) p. 44; popicon (get perspective icon) pgs. 57, 60, 62, 64, 66, 74, 76, 80, 82, 84, 90, 108, 112, 115, 118, 120; rungrote (baby) p. 44; simpleblues (globe) p. 44; Skylines (tune in icon) pgs. 56, 64, 70, 72, 74, 80, 82, 96, 98, 100, 104, 106, 108, 118, 120; Texturis (gnome) p. 44; vectuz (weightlifter) p. 44; Yasna Ten (soothe icon) pgs. 56, 62, 66, 74, 80, 82, 88, 90, 92, 96, 98, 100, 104, 106, 108, 112, 115

CONTENTS

STRESS: AN INTRODUCTION

Once upon a time, there was a royal who lived in a nice castle in a nice kingdom where everyone was nice and nothing bad ever happened. The end.

Wake up! Wow, that was boring. Really, it was probably the most painfully boring nonstory possible. What makes stories—and life—interesting and meaningful is challenge, risk, tension, and resolution. Facing fears and learning lessons. Trying hard, failing, looking like an idiot, trying again. People *not* being nice to each other all day every day. Of course, all that mess causes stress (at least for most of us). And stress doesn't always feel nice, does it?

Well, that's just part of the deal. You might as well accept the fact that stress is everywhere, always, and forever. It's not going anywhere. You can never escape! But that's better than living in some shiny-happy utopian snoozefest, right? **SO GET OVER IT.**

HOW TO USE THIS BOOK

In these pages, we'll take a look at this mysterious, catchall category of life that we generally label as "stress." This includes:

- The experience, as in what stress actually feels like
- Different types of stress
- How ongoing stress affects us

We'll also look at the many ways to manage stress, with step-by-step instructions that are relatively easy to follow.

DISCLAIMER

This book is in absolutely no way the ultimate authority on how to handle stress. The people who made this book are not doctors or therapists. Honestly, if you saw them, your first question would be, *I'm supposed to get advice from these hot messes?* followed closely by, *Do they not have hairbrushes where they live?* Ergo, if you are struggling, reach out to someone you trust so they can help you get care.

PART ONE

#STRESSED

FEELING STRESSED YET?

Stress is that super-annoying thing that happens when life isn't handed to you on a silver platter. You know, when you have other people's expectations to deal with and deadlines to meet, and your teeth aren't going to brush themselves, and your brother's a jerk.

Simply put, stress is the pressure you feel—physically, mentally, and emotionally—when you're worried or overwhelmed. Of course, there isn't a one-size-fits-all kind of stress in life. (Isn't that great?)

There are many sides to this stress situation, as in:

- The mind/body experience, sometimes rudely called "symptoms"
- "Negative" stress versus "positive" stress—yes, positive stress is a thing
- Types of stress that happen rarely and unexpectedly (acute), occasionally but expectedly (episodic), or all the freaking time (chronic)

And stress makes us *do* stuff to get it to go away. Depending on the stress and the person, it could prompt us to work harder, hide under the covers, bite our nails, or eat a whole bag of potato chips while shaking our fists at the universe and screaming "Why?!"

UNHELPFUL ADVICE

~~JUST BE YOUR-SELF~~

Um, OK. Could you maybe be a little more specific?

POP QUIZ

HOW STRESSED ARE YOU?

Write down your answers for each question, and add up your total score at the end.

In the last month, how often have you:

Felt like you were locked inside a box inside a barrel shot out of a cannon into the middle of the ocean?

1. Never
2. Sometimes
3. Often
4. Every other Tuesday
5. 100 percent of the time

Spent hours online railing against the tyranny of something pretty standard, like shoelaces or rain clouds?

1. Never
2. Once or twice
3. Often
4. At teatime
5. Nonstop

Felt like screaming your lungs out or threatening grievous bodily harm to an inanimate object?

1. Never
2. Occasionally
3. Frequently
4. Every morning
5. *Ahhhhhhhhhhhhhhhhhhhhhhh!*

Believed in your heart of hearts that the cat/dog/squirrel/ murder of crows/pygmy goat/ alligator across the street is judging you?

1. Never
2. Rarely
3. Frequently
4. Always
5. If you saw the look in their eyes, you'd say *Always* too

HOW TO SCORE

Add up your answers. Your stress level is:

4 to 7 = Warm turquoise water lapping at your toes as you sip guava juice on a white sandy beach.

8 to 11 = You're eating a sandwich and the tomato falls out, but it's mostly OK because you don't like tomatoes out of season that much anyway.

12 to 14 = Your crush since, like, kindergarten has just appeared at your door, but you just rolled out of bed and also the fire alarm is going off.

15 to 17 = Is it normal for this car to make that sort of rattly gravel-in-a-dryer sound? Hey, watch out for that line of ducklings crossing the road!

18 to 20 = You are a figment of a giant's imagination, and that giant is having a wicked nightmare about being chased by spiders through hot lava while naked on the red carpet at the Academy Awards.

No matter what you scored today, stress is a fact of life that will build and release and affect you every day. So buckle up, Buttercup: it's about to get real.

ALL THE FEELS

What does it actually *feel* like when you are stressed? You, my dear, are a glorious onion, with many layers for enjoying all the complexity that stress has to offer. You are mind and body, thoughts and emotions, and sensations and reactions.

Of course, there's no real distinction between all the parts that make you you. For our purposes, however, we'll divvy you up into four categories of "symptoms." These are:

1. **Physical or physiological:** where and how stress shows up in your body
2. **Emotional or psychological:** how stress affects your feelings and your mood
3. **Cognitive or mental:** how stress influences your thinking and perceptions
4. **Behavioral or you-doing-stuff:** how stress affects the way you act

Ready for the absolute *best* part? Stress often manifests in *many* symptoms, *all at the same time*. Great. Let's take a closer peek at what those symptoms might look and feel like.

It's Normal!

To be unsure what stress actually is

To be confused about the difference between sensations/feelings/thoughts

To wish you could punch stress right in the face

PHYSICAL/ PHYSIOLOGICAL SYMPTOMS

Having a body can be a huge hassle. First of all, you have to clean it about nine different ways. Sometimes it gets sick and gross stuff comes out of it. You must drape it with various textiles to protect it from the weather and hide the private bits. And don't even get me started on the hair (see earlier disclaimer)!

But it also does amazing things. It moves and digests food and sings in the shower. It breathes and grows and lugs your brain from place to place. And it has all kinds of sensations.

What does stress feel like in the physical body?

Headaches
Tightness in the chest or shallow breathing
Upset stomach
Being tired
Being wired
Sweating
Racing heartbeat
Sleeping too much
Sleeping not enough
Getting sick
Dizziness or disorientation
Muscle tenseness or soreness
Teeth grinding or clenching your jaw
Bull-like nostril flaring
Random itchiness
Single-eye twitching

Where do YOU feel the stress in your body? What are the sensations YOU associate with stress ?

UNHELPFUL ADVICE

~~IF THERE'S A WILL, THERE'S A WAY.~~

Cool cool cool.
But what if I'm, like, really tired?

EMOTIONAL/PSYCHOLOGICAL SYMPTOMS

Remember how we said that stress can manifest in many symptoms at the same time? Emotional/psychological symptoms almost never go it alone. An emotional experience can be thought of as a bodily sensation plus thoughts. For example, you notice a tingly sensation in your legs. You think, *I'm feeling nervous*. Or you think, *Ugh! Why is everyone being so stupid today?* while clenching your jaw so tightly you chip a tooth. (Irritable much?) You get the picture: physical stress symptoms and emotional stress symptoms go hand in hand.

What sort of feelings are associated with stress?

Nervousness
Worry
Irritability
Frustration
Seriously-over-itness
Restlessness
Numbness
Apathy
Forgetfulness
Spaciness
Don't-tell-me-what-to-doishness
Existential dread

What are the emotions YOU have that go along with stress? What emotions cause stress ?

COGNITIVE/MENTAL SYMPTOMS

Though grinding teeth or being tired/wired can be a drag, physical symptoms like these actually serve as signposts. If you check in with that racing heart or churning stomach, you might discover that it's pointing you toward cognitive/mental symptoms you hadn't yet noticed—or vice versa. Some people tend to be more aware of what's happening in their minds, while others tend to be more aware of what's happening in their bodies.

For example, not being able to fall asleep might pair with constantly replaying that mortifying moment when you realized your zipper was down during your presentation, or overwhelming fatigue comes with having too much homework on top of a swim meet on top of your friend having a meltdown over the dent in their new water bottle. These symptoms squat in your mind and often come with words, or an inner monologue, though not always.

What kinds of thoughts do YOU associate with stress? What kinds of thoughts might cause stress?

How does stress show up in the mind?

Indecisiveness
Repetitive thinking, usually about stuff that makes you feel bad and goes nowhere
Incessant worry about the future
Replaying painful memories
Constantly interpreting events or interactions in a negative light
Forgetfulness
Difficulty focusing
Lack of motivation
Continuously brainstorming stress solutions that usually involve buying stuff or decluttering all that stuff you just bought

How does negativity bias show up in YOUR life? What have YOU been hypervigilant about ?

WHAT IS NEGATIVITY BIAS?

When you're stressed, are you a total Negative Nancy? That's actually a good thing—if humans were still cave people. Focusing on the negative is likely a survival mechanism: your brain remembers when something bad happens and recognizes patterns that could keep you safe from, like, marauding grizzlies and poison berries. It's not as helpful when it comes to something like public speaking or fighting with your bestie.

Seriously, our little brains don't know when to give it a rest. We end up fixating on minor frictions, or transforming something uncomfortable into a catastrophe, like when we accidentally snarted in the grocery store. While occasional fixation is a fact of being human, done too often, it can turn into the habit of hypervigilance, or constantly preparing for bad stuff to happen and basically assuming everyone is terrible and everything is ruined. That's definitely not a fun way to live.

BEHAVIORAL/YOU-DOING-STUFF SYMPTOMS

Every action has a reaction, and unless you're *super* on top of it, sensations/thoughts/emotions spark reactions, a.k.a. behaviors. Often, when we're stressed, we act without making a conscious choice—we feel like we *need* to do something, even if we know that what we do might not serve us (like snapping at a friend). Reactions are not inherently "bad." They can be signposts alerting you that stress is at it again, and it might be time to assess your options.

How do we behave when we're stressed?

Difficulty sleeping
Procrastination
Nail-biting
Crying
Compulsions like excessive handwashing, skin picking, eating past the point of satiation
Pacing
Lashing out
Avoiding potentially stressful situations
Shopping and gambling
Face-palming
Streaming whatever the it reality show of the moment is

Are there certain things YOU do when you get stressed? Even if you don't actually *do* anything, do YOU have certain impulses when stressed

?

FOR EXAMPLE: SYMPTOMS IRL

Imagine you've been assigned an essay for your English class, due next Friday. Your teacher hands out the assignment on a sheet of paper. As you read about what you have to do, you:

Feel a tightening in your chest (Physical symptom)

Feel overwhelmed (Emotional symptom)

Think thoughts like *This is too hard. I hate writing. I have too much to do already. I'm tired. When's lunch?* (Cognitive symptom)

Shove the assignment into the dark pit of your backpack, hoping it'll disappear forever (Behavioral symptom)

Imagine your parents telling you that you need to get an after-school job. As you think about what you have to do, you:

Feel churning in your stomach (Physical symptom)

Feel annoyed (Emotional symptom)

Think thoughts like *I don't want to. Who would hire me? I don't even know where to begin!* (Cognitive symptom)

Tell your parents that you'll look but keep putting it off (Behavioral symptom)

Imagine you and your friend got into a major fight, and neither of you has apologized yet. As you picture seeing them tomorrow at work, you:

Feel your palms start to sweat (Physical symptom)

Feel nervous (Emotional symptom)

Think thoughts like *I don't know if we can be friends again. I can't stand this!* (Cognitive symptom)

Plan to call in sick tomorrow, just to put it off another day (Behavioral symptom)

UNHELPFUL ADVICE

~~TRUST YOUR GUT.~~

But what if my gut is telling me to throw up, then crawl under my bed and never come out?

POP QUIZ

HOW DO YOU EXPERIENCE STRESS?

You forgot to take out the trash after you were told, repeatedly, to do so. Your parent/roommate/dog/inner critic proceeds to yell at you. What do you notice first about your experience?

A) You get sweaty and your chest feels tight.
B) You feel sad and guilty and angry and disgusted.
C) You think about how they don't understand you, or care.
D) You cry.
E) All of the above.

Your teacher asks you to stay after class. Why? You have no idea. What do you notice first about your experience?

A) Your throat feels constricted.
B) You feel afraid and preemptively defensive.
C) You start mentally spiraling into worst-case scenarios.
D) You bite your nails down to the quick or can't stop fidgeting.
E) All of the above.

Your best friend drops some unexpected bad news: they're going to move away next month. What do you notice first about your experience?

A) Your entire body goes numb.
B) You feel . . . nothing.
C) Your mind goes blank.
D) Your jaw drops and you can't muster the energy to close it.
E) All of the above.

You go to the spot where you parked your car/bike/scooter/unicycle/skateboard/hot-air balloon only to discover that . . . it's not there. What do you notice first about your experience?

A) Your shoulders tense and electric zaps shoot down your arms.
B) You feel confused and disoriented.
C) A series of possibilities race through your head at lightning speed.
D) You spin around, scanning the environment for criminal elements.
E) All of the above.

YOU KEY

If you chose mostly A's, then you tend to first notice physical symptoms.

If you chose mostly B's, then you tend to first notice emotional symptoms.

If you chose mostly C's, then you tend to first notice mental symptoms.

If you chose mostly D's, then you tend to first notice behavioral symptoms.

If you chose mostly E's, or a combo of A's, B's, C's, and D's, then you are pretty clued in to your stress signals. BRAVO.

PAIN AND GAIN

The thing is, we need stress. Your bones grow and your muscles get stronger by stressing them with weight and motion—without that, they atrophy. Likewise, you need challenges to learn, improve, expand—without that, we'd all just sit around sucking our thumbs and waiting for someone else to take care of things. Which is an option, I guess. But it's not cute.

BUSTED!

STRESS MYTHS DEBUNKED

"Stress leads to poor performance."

What, you think elite performers aren't stressed?

Of course they're stressed. Being awesome is stressful. Yet somehow they figure out how to channel that stress into getting the job done.

I STRESS, YOU STRESS, DISTRESS

Stress comes in two flavors: eustress and distress. Eustress may be hard, but it is manageable and contained. It's usually tied to a specific challenge related to a larger goal and has the potential for reward. Take, for example, a math test, which is a finite stressor happening only next Thursday during second period and related to the goal of you not being a total ditz. The reward is you getting a decent grade and feeling a sense of accomplishment.

On the other hand, too much challenge and too much stress can be . . . too much. Too much weight or too much motion can break bones or injure muscles. And too much stress on you can cause distress, which feels overwhelming or destabilizing or just baaaaaaad. Distress often shows up when we experience a lack of control.

EUSTRESS OR DISTRESS?

It's not always easy to tell distress from eustress. What feels bad today might feel less bad tomorrow, but that doesn't necessarily mean it is an overall positive. Then again, what feels bad today might lead to bigger and better things, make us stronger, or give us the insight needed to make healthier choices in the future. Maybe. Hopefully. At least every once in a while?

KNOW YOUR STRESS

EUSTRESS = Motivating stress that helps you focus on a task—yay!

DISTRESS = Demotivating stress that makes it hard for you to achieve success (or much of anything sometimes)—boo!

FOR EXAMPLE: SITUATIONS IRL

A history test

Distress in the moment → expands your view of the world and moves you forward academically or highlights an area in which you need help

Constant drama at home

Ongoing distress → leads you to therapy, education around interpersonal communication and mental health, and other helpful (though difficult) strategies for taking care of yourself

A breakup or rejection

Distress in the moment → until you meet someone new or find a new passion and reinterpret that breakup/rejection as one (mis)step along the path of romance or self-discovery

UNHELPFUL ADVICE

~~EVERY CLOUD HAS A SILVER LINING.~~

Every *single* cloud?
C'mon. That is absolutely, definitively not true. It's, like, statistically impossible.

SITUATIONS + HUMANS + TIME = TYPES OF STRESS

Life loves to throw different kinds of stress at you. You know, to keep you on your toes. Forever. Super cool, Life. Really, thanks a lot.

There are three overarching ways that stressors show up in real time in your life.

Acute stress is sudden, unexpected, and intense. These are the events that you don't see coming but have a big impact. The surprise adds to the stress. **FOR EXAMPLE:**

- Your partner dumps you out of the blue
- Someone you care about dies suddenly
- You get into a car accident
- Your parent loses their job
- A natural disaster hits your community

Episodic stress is finite and expected. It's related to an event that's common or regular enough to be on the calendar. You know it's coming, and sometimes the anticipation adds to the stress. **FOR EXAMPLE:**

- Project deadlines
- Dentist and doctor appointments
- The pulsating zit you get once a month so consistently that you could set a watch to it

- A first date
- School dances and other social events
- Sports matches, theater/dance/choir/band performances, art shows
- Tryouts, auditions, or job interviews
- Having to wear an ugly holiday sweater and take photos with your extended family

Chronic stress is ongoing and deeply rooted. These are stressful situations that happen regularly and yet are unpredictable, and they can make life feel chaotic and out of control. **FOR EXAMPLE:**

- Being bullied
- Family members arguing at home
- Continual financial strain and lack of access to opportunity or resources
- Ongoing health issues that make daily functioning difficult
- Crime in your community
- All forms of systemic and personal discrimination

DIS/REGULATION

The body has a basic stress-management protocol that works fine . . . except when the hits keep coming without any kind of relief. If you don't get a chance to recover, your internal resources get overly taxed. This results in burnout, feelings of nervousness or sadness, and vulnerability to illness or injury.

This is why we need to *actively do* stress management, because the body's natural abilities only go so far when facing chronic stress. Why? Because your body is a very, very, very imperfect machine.

PART TWO

BLOOD-THIRSTY LIONS AND OTHER RELATABLE STRESSOR EXAMPLES

PICTURE THIS

You're walking through the jungle. By your side is your trusty spear, which you've named Sir Jabs. Birds are chirping, monkeys are hooting, and somewhere far away, a waterfall goes whoosh. Suddenly, silence. Is it your imagination, or did a cloud just pass over the sun?

Up ahead and to the right, there's rustling, then a lion steps onto the path. She's got a hungry look in her eyes. You look down at yourself and think, *Ugh! I* am *a tasty snack*. Quite unsubtly, she licks her chops. What do you do? *WHAT DO YOU DO?*

BUSTED!

STRESS MYTHS DEBUNKED

"We are more stressed out today than we've ever been."

How would we even know that?

Not having central heating or hunting antelopes with bow and arrow was probably pretty stressful, actually.

Most of us won't ever encounter this particular scenario, but our ancestors did (or something like it). What these ancient people did in that moment had big consequences—they were either eaten by lions or they survived long enough to make some babies and become ancestors. The ones who made the babies are our great-great-great-to-the-fifty-eighth-degree-grandparents. If they could see us now, they'd be so proud!

Nowadays, our lions probably aren't actually lions. (Or maybe yours are—no judgment!) We've still got survival-level problems, like speeding cars and falling pianos. We also have loads of lesser problems that often still *feel* like lions, and we respond to them as if they were lions. We **fight**, take **flight**, **freeze**, or **fawn**.

Stress responses are neither good nor bad. Sometimes the behavior is adaptive; sometimes it's maladaptive. Sometimes it helps; sometimes it harms.

FIGHT

The lion—let's call her Nancy—crouches. You crouch. "Sir Jabs," you whisper through clenched teeth, looking at the spear in your hand, "I love you very much. Now, on your guard." Nancy rears back, preparing to spring. You do the same. *Kablam!* You are full-on fighting a bloodthirsty lion!

IRL: SENSATION SEEKING

In modern terms, the fight response is when your body gets ready to attack. This can take the form of literal physical fighting or lashing out verbally. Most of us, however, have been conditioned to repress and transform that urge into more "acceptable" forms than punching, for better or worse. This includes sensation-seeking and thrill-seeking—as in, searching for experiences that are new or intense and give you big feelings, positive or negative.

CHEAP THRILL

HOLD YOUR BREATH

. . . for as long as you can. Scary, right? Don't worry, your tricky little brain won't let you get hurt!

What, if any, fight responses do YOU have ?

Sensation-seeking examples:

- Anger and frustration
- Physical or verbal fighting, obvi
- Standing up for yourself, someone else, or a cause you believe in
- Clenching jaw or teeth grinding
- Destroying property
- Crying
- Feeling hot and uncomfortable
- Getting competitive and actively pursuing goals
- Seeking out intense altered states, like those that come from extreme physical exertion or pain, **FOR EXAMPLE:**
    - Running marathons
    - Getting tattoos and piercings
    - Eating crazy-hot peppers
- Taking risks, **FOR EXAMPLE:**
    - Race car driving
    - Skydiving
    - Cliff jumping
    - Gambling
    - Dyeing your hair purple
    - Composing a song about how you hate your dad

FLIGHT

Nancy the lion crouches. You crouch. Nancy smiles, like, actually smiles. Your heart rate skyrockets. "C'mon, Sir Jabs!" you say as you take off, sprinting as fast as you can through the jungle.

IRL: AVOIDANCE

Unless you are literally running away from an oncoming truck, today the flight response takes the form of escaping a stressful situation by more subtle means. Sometimes you physically leave a scary interaction; sometimes you leave only in your mind, because you are unable to literally flee. You have developed a sensitivity to certain situations and respond by floating away to la-la land, or you'd rather check TikTok than do your homework.

What, if any, flight responses do YOU have?

Avoidance-response examples:

- Restlessness, feeling trapped
- Fidgeting
- Cutting ties with mean people
- Saying no
- Turning down invitations to parties
- Refusing to try new things
- Excessive exercising
- Isolating yourself so you don't have to deal with parents/people
- Procrastination/distraction, a.k.a. doing just about

BUSTED!

STRESS MYTHS DEBUNKED

"Procrastination is a sign of laziness."

Procrastination can stem from all kinds of issues, like perfectionism, fear of failure, lack of motivation, or feeling overwhelmed.

I'm not lazy—your myth is lazy!

anything to avoid something that is hard, unpleasant, or scary, like doing the dishes or confronting a friend about that thing they did that hurt your feelings, **FOR EXAMPLE:**

- Checking social media a thousand times a day
- Overscheduling or overcommitting yourself
- Ignoring emails
- Wearing your underwear inside out so you don't have to do laundry for another day
- Putting off making decisions until the very last minute
- Starting a big project at 10:00 p.m. the night before it's due
- Waiting to pursue a big goal or dream until everything's perfect and you feel 100 percent ready and confident

FREEZE

Nancy the lion crouches. You don't move. You can't move! It's like your body is frozen in place. You can sense Sir Jab's frustration. Nancy just looks confused. Possibly, maybe, hopefully she's thinking that you don't seem like such a tasty snack after all?

IRL: DISSOCIATION

The freeze response is associated with dissociation, or "checking out." Chronic stress tends to bring out this response over time, especially if it comes from a sense of helplessness or lack of control. If you are constantly involved in family drama, or you are exposed to

BUSTED!

STRESS MYTHS DEBUNKED

"Feeling stressed is a sign of weakness."

Actually, acknowledging you feel stressed is the first step toward managing it.

That's pretty darn strong, huh?

marginalization day in and day out, you might learn, consciously or unconsciously, that giving up is the easiest course of action, at least in the short term. There's nothing you can do, says your subconscious, so you do nothing. You sit there and wait for it to be over.

Dissociation-response examples:

- Tight chest
- Lightheadedness or dizziness
- Numbness, coldness, heaviness
- Feeling disconnected from the body, having an "out of body" experience
- Feeling stuck or stiff
- Mental blankness, being at a loss for words
- Spacing out
- Daydreaming
- Having a sense of dread or hopelessness
- Being apathetic
- Forgetting things
- Feeling indecisive and passive, FOR EXAMPLE:
    - Really, truly feeling like you have no opinion on simple matters, like what to eat for lunch
    - Being more comfortable with other people making decisions for you
    - Frequently choosing a supportive role in relationships
    - Doing nothing until you are forced to or the decision is made for you
    - Not caring what happens to you
    - Not defending yourself
    - Going with the flow

What, if any, freeze responses do YOU have to stress?

FAWN

Nancy crouches. You smile your friendliest smile. "Hey, girl!" you say, "Your fur is slaying the day away! Plus, simply wow, those muscles. I mean, could they *be* any stronger? And those teeth? So white! Tell me, what's your secret?"

IRL: VIGILANCE

OK, fine, that's preposterous. But fawning as a survival response is a real and often reasonable one, particularly when dealing with people who have, or whom we perceive to have, more power than we do. You essentially suck up in an effort to please and appease.

Vigilance-response examples:

- People-pleasing
- Trying to be overly helpful
- Overextending yourself
- Overachieving
- Fixating
- Generally being an eager beaver
- Prioritizing others' wants and needs over your own
- Agreeing with someone, even if you have a different idea
- Saying yes all the time

What, if any, fawn responses do YOU have to stress?

- Valuing others' opinions over your own
- Having issues with boundaries
- Being vulnerable to manipulation
- Being a perfectionist, **FOR EXAMPLE:**
    - Feeling incapable of letting go of control
    - Having rigid beliefs around what's correct and what's not
    - Constantly worrying over what you perceive as mistakes or failures
    - Being a harsh self-critic and having untenable expectations
    - Believing (falsely) that you can control everything and win love through accomplishment or perfect performance
    - Internalizing stigma against a group to which you belong
    - Being disconnected from your own authentic wants and needs
    - Being successful (sorry, it's true!)

Any of these responses

It's Normal!

All of them

POP QUIZ

HOW DO YOU RESPOND TO STRESS?

Someone makes fun of you for random nonsense every couple of weeks. Let's call her Gegina Shmorge. How do you respond?

A) You flick her earlobe and call her "Ms. Annoying" in front of all her friends.
B) You run out of the room and cry in a bathroom stall.
C) You smile awkwardly and think about what's for dinner later.
D) You say, "Oh my, Gegina Shmorge! You're so funny!"
E) All of the above.

Your bus slides on black ice and ends up in a ditch. Everyone's fine, but it was scary. How do you respond?

A) You tell the driver that he needs to get his eyes checked and go back to driving school. Then you go skydiving.
B) You act like everything is fine while your mind floats a million feet above your body.
C) You can't move, and a firefighter has to basically carry you off the bus.
D) You offer to help every single person off the bus, all while giving a pep talk to cheer everyone up.
E) All of the above.

You have a big, huge, life-altering deadline coming up. How do you respond?

A) You yell at your sister, her partner, a puppy, your best friend, and the TV.
B) You wait until 12:02 a.m. the day it's due to start working on it.
C) You sit down to work on it every day, but often find yourself daydreaming about which superpower you'd choose if given the choice.
D) You work on it regularly and make good progress, but you can't sleep at night because you're so worried about it being absolutely perfect in every way.
E) All of the above.

You have a two-hundred-year-old great cousin twice removed who makes some snide passive-aggressive comment about "the youth" at every family function. She's headed this way. How do you respond?

A) Preemptively ask a snide question about what it was like riding dinosaurs to school back in her day.
B) Jump behind a potted plant and pray she didn't see you.
C) Hum under your breath while staring off into space until she gets bored and leaves.
D) Say, "You make a good point" to every hurtful, ridiculous thing she says.
E) All of the above.

YOU KEY

If you chose mostly A's, then you tend to fight.

If you chose mostly B's, then you tend toward flight.

If you chose mostly C's, then you tend to freeze.

If you chose mostly D's, then you tend to fawn.

If you chose mostly E's, or a combo of A's, B's, C's, and D's, then you are a human person.

PART THREE

THANK GOODNESS IT'S EVERYONE ELSE'S FAULT

BLAME GRANDMA: GENES, FAMILY NONSENSE, AND THE ENTIRE WORLD

Looking for someone to blame for your stress? Start with Grandma. While you're at it, blame Grandpa. Both grandpas. And all great-great-great-grandpas and great-great-great-grandmas. Blame your parents too, obvi. But don't stop there. Blame society and culture. Blame famines of yesteryear, wars and pandemics, and all the bad things that made life hard for your predecessors. Of course, blame the tough stuff that happened not so long ago, in your early childhood, at home and abroad.

How lovely it is to have someones and somethings to blame! Let's call this epigenetics lite, a.k.a. the theory that what makes you YOU is a roiling storm of factors, internal and external, multigenerational and multidimensional. It comes from inside your body and outside in the world, which aren't as separate as we might perceive.

In short, you are born into this world a crying, drooling smooshy-smooshface of potential. You have around twenty thousand genes, half from bio-mom and half from bio-dad, and each of these genes is like a little blueprint for traits. Some traits are pretty much set, like eye color, and some are more impressionable—they can get turned "on" or "off" via input from your environment. Take height: if your parents are both as tall as two redwoods, then there's a good chance you'll be tall too. But if you don't get proper nutrition or you have a serious childhood illness, that *potential* for tallness may not present itself.

BUSTED!

STRESS MYTHS DEBUNKED

"Stress is caused solely by external factors."

Sure, external factors like work pressure or friend-group problems contribute to stress, but internal factors like unrealistic expectations and negative self-talk certainly don't help!

GENES

(those itty-bitty pieces of DNA inherited from your bio-parents that guide development)

+

EXPERIENCES & ENVIRONMENT

(everything that happens to and around you, negative and positive)

=

YOU

Here's how all of that plays into stress. You know those people who seem chill all the time? Like nothing ever rattles them? Like they take bad news and good news in stride, like they can shake off stuff that would really bug you? Maybe it's because they meditate for two hours a day and eat only kale-spirulina-avocado smoothies. Or it might be part of their natural disposition, combined with experiences—both positive and negative—that promote higher stress tolerance.

If that's you, then **WHY ARE YOU EVEN HERE?** Go find your own self-help book that's all about being so chill you're bored or something.

It's Normal!

To be bothered

To be unbothered

To wish there was a single thing you could blame for everything

AHEM.

Back to blaming Grandma. Let's say your predecessors had an average share of exposure to stressful experiences—crop failures, various poxes, lack of indoor plumbing, et cetera. On top of that, their familial and cultural styles of dealing with stress weren't very healthy, at least not as judged by today's standards (though they did accomplish the biological imperative of survival, so yay for them!). Maybe they were taught to expect the worst and shut up about it, or to lash out at those around them. Whatever their method, this got passed down the family line. And unless your parents did a crazy amount of therapy and self-work to kick all those heirloom habits, they made their way to you.

Then you, personally, faced your own set of stressors within your specific environment. Maybe you've experienced significant upheaval or chronic health issues. Maybe your household has drama. Maybe there are big systemic challenges in your community. Your experiences within this environment combine with your genes to form the strange combo meal that is you, including your stress tolerance baseline and stress response.

Wait! Don't close this book and throw it out the window. You do have (some) control. All of the above is simply reality, not destiny.

UNHELPFUL ADVICE

~~ALL YOU HAVE TO DO IS CHOOSE TO BE HAPPY.~~

Bless your heart.
That's a bald-faced
lie and you know it.

THE STORY OF YOU

Ask yourself the following questions.
(Even better, write down your answers.)

1. What can you find out about your ancestors' hardships and struggles to survive? This could be fleeing war, immigrating to a strange new land, living in poverty, abusing alcohol, being oppressed, et cetera.
2. What can you find out about how your ancestors dealt with hardship? In other words, what were their responses to stress?
3. What stories have you heard from your community (however you define that: your religious community, your ethnic or racial group, your political party, etc.) about earlier generations' hardships and struggles to survive?
4. How did your community deal with hardship? What were some cultural narratives or practices around managing stress?

UNHELPFUL ADVICE

NO PAIN. NO GAIN.

No, thank you!

5. What stories do your individual family members tell about their personal hardships and struggles to survive in their own lives?
6. How do your family members currently deal with hardships and manage stress? If you aren't sure, ask them. (And if they can't or won't answer, that, too, is interesting information. Isn't it?)
7. What stories have you heard from your community about its more recent hardships and struggles to survive?
8. How does your community, as a whole and as individual members, currently deal with hardships and manage stress? If you aren't sure, ask. (And if people can't or won't answer, that's interesting information; hmm?)

Go over your answers. How does what you know or learned about your family, community, and history help you understand your own responses to stress?

PART FOUR

THE NEVER-ENDING MAINTENANCE OF EXISTENCE

STRESS-BE-GONE INSTANT RELIEF TRICKS!

OK, this stress thing is real. Fortunately for you, here are some stress-relief tips and tricks that will absolutely 100 percent fix your stress every single time. You'll never have problems again!

Wait. What? You mean, that's not how it works? Oh, shoot. So what you're saying is you have to try out a stress-relief trick and see what happens, and probably do it a bunch of times? And then, something that used to work stops working, so you have to try out other things, probably a bunch of times? For your entire life? Ugh. So much work.

FIND YOUR OWN STRESS ANTIDOTE

The following section offers some ideas for stress management. It's a mix-and-match menu, a choose-your-own-de-stressing adventure.

Things you can do to de-stress include:

- Empathize
- Investigate
- Organize
- Rest
- Breathe
- Move
- Laugh
- Unplug

It's Normal!

To want a quick fix

To get annoyed at yourself for not being better at this

To make the mistake of trusting a stress-relief guru who promises to cure you for the low, low price of $999.99

POP QUIZ

WHAT'S YOUR DE-STRESSOR STYLE?

Out of the following stress management techniques, which do you choose:

When repeatedly faced with the same type of problem?

A) Talk to a friend about why it keeps happening.
B) Listen to a guided meditation while taking a bubble bath.
C) Throw on your favorite unitard and YouTube a 1980s workout video.
D) Look online for something you can buy to help you with this issue.
E) All of the above.

When overwhelmed by the boring obligations of life?

A) Read a book about someone struggling with the boring obligations of life (sounds like a real page-turner!)
B) Make a checklist of a thousand things you have to do from now through forever.
C) Put on a gray sweat suit and re-create that endless jogging scene from *Rocky*.
D) Go down a Wiki rabbit hole for three to six hours.
E) All of the above.

When asked out of the blue to do something that challenges/ terrifies you?

A) Write a letter to future you, describing your current experience and giving yourself a motivational speech.
B) Build a pillow fort and take a deliciously cozy nap.
C) Watch fail videos until you laugh so hard you pee your pants.
D) Scroll.
E) All of the above.

YOU KEY

If you chose mostly A's, check out Empathize, Investigate, or Organize.

If you chose mostly B's, check out Organize, Rest, or Breathe.

If you chose mostly C's, check out Breathe, Move, or Laugh.

If you chose mostly D's, check out Unplug.

If you chose mostly E's, or a combo of A's, B's, C's, and D's, check out all of them. Actually, do that anyway.

Along with step-by-step instructions, each practice includes an at-a-glance dashboard so you can see which kind of management method it falls under. These stress reduction methods include Tune In, Soothe, Redirect, and Get Perspective.

TUNE IN

Way back in 1914, Robert Frost wrote "the best way out is always through." Which is true for things over which you have little control. Sometimes you just have to go through *it*, to simply sit with *it*, notice *it*, allow *it*, observe *it*, maybe even accept *it*, and wait. For what it's worth, this method sucks, discomfort-wise. But it's also mandatory sometimes, so you might as well learn how to do it.

SOOTHE

Remember when you were little and you got a boo-boo on your knee, and all you needed was someone to give you a hug or a kiss to make you feel better? You are now both the boo-boo haver and the hug-and-kiss giver. Strategies here are direct responses, like aloe on a sunburn.

CHEAP THRILL

WATCH PAINT DRY.

That low-intensity, top-tier boredom will make doing literally anything else feel amazing.

REDIRECT

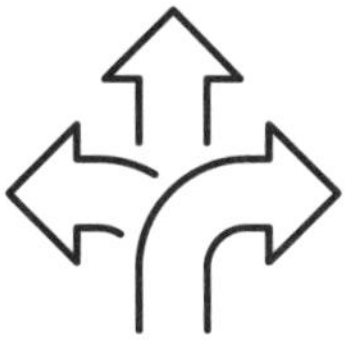

Sometimes pointing your focus away from what's stressing you out is your best bet. Instead of sitting with those feelings and thoughts or dealing with them directly, put your attention elsewhere—watch a movie, call a friend, dance like nobody's watching.

GET PERSPECTIVE

Sometimes what we need is a little broadening of our horizons, a glimpse into the wider world to see that we're not alone in our struggles and that other people have problems too. Perspective isn't meant to make you feel guilty or ashamed, or to turn you into some kind of trauma tourist. Rather, it frees you from that stuck place in the center of the universe.

Empathize

. . . or Stress-Relief Tactics That Make Your Heart Feel All Warm and Gooey Like a Marshmallow in the Microwave

Empathy is the ability to understand someone else's feelings, to use your imagination to step into their size 14 bedazzled Crocs. Doing so gives us a break from the self-centeredness baked into stress and worry. Without diminishing or dismissing your experience, or taking on other people's baggage, you can give yourself a break from your internal focus and peek through a window into other possibilities.

WHY EMPATHIZE?

1. **Empathy is a prosocial skill.** Developing it can help you make friends and improve relationships, which can grant you social cachet, which can move forward your goal of world domination, which in turn can relieve stress.

2. **Empathy's close cousin, compassion, has the added ingredient of concern for others' suffering.** Empathy and compassion can motivate you to take action toward making the world a better place.

3. **Empathy is a brain exercise.** Without it, your brain gets all flabby and weak. You don't want a flabby, weak brain—do you?

READ A NOVEL

WHY SHOULD I?

Reading fiction is one of the best ways to develop emotional intelligence, open-mindedness, and creativity. By getting inside someone else's story, you step outside your own teeny-tiny experience. You see that different people have very different lives, that we don't all see and feel the world the same way, and that it's possible to fall in love with a vampire-sorceress-snake, no matter how many walls you put up around your heart.

TRY THIS

- When you're caught up in your drama
- When you're feeling sorry for yourself
- When you've been banished from screens

HOW

1. Learn how to read.
2. Choose a book that you and only you—not your teachers, not your parents, not your friends or social media—are interested in. Could be anything. Doesn't have to be a thousand pages long. It just has to have pages.
3. Read it.

UNHELPFUL ADVICE

DON'T TAKE IT PERSON-ALLY.

I mean, how else am I supposed to take something that is affecting me as a person?

BABY VISUALIZATION

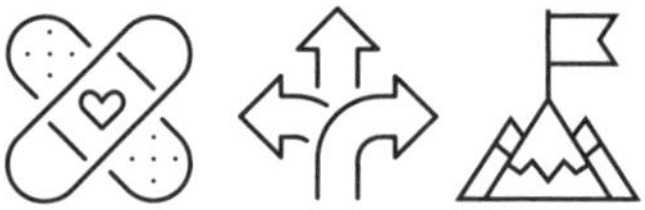

WHY SHOULD I?

Every single person, whether they are the meanest bully, the most uptight adult, or the huge stress-ball that is you, used to be a baby. A sweet-smelling, dewy-cheeked little baby, born innocent and adorable into an imperfect world that immediately made its mark and ultimately turned them into a mean/nagging/stressed human. Remember, they're just like you.

TRY THIS

- When you are feeling extra blamey toward a specific individual (including yourself)
- When you're in the mood to be kinda cheesy
- Just because babies are cute, especially when you don't have to change their diapers

HOW

1. Close your eyes or do a very slow blink.
2. Think about the person you're mad at/irritated by.
3. Imagine that person as a baby. Can you picture them without all that hair and attitude, pore enlargement and sense of entitlement, body odor and mean streak? Can you picture them in a giraffe-patterned onesie or some other snuggly-wuggly outfit? Can you picture them kicking their squishy little baby legs while grinning at you with a gummy smile?
4. Imagine holding them (or yourself) in your arms, rocking them gently, singing a lullaby. Imagine soothing this perfect little baby who only wants to be warm and fed and safe and loved.

BUSTED!

STRESS MYTHS DEBUNKED

"Stress causes gray hair."

No. Age causes gray hair.
And a whole bunch of other issues.

ASSUME THE BEST

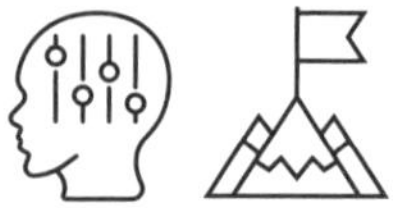

WHY SHOULD I?

We tend to assume other people's obnoxiousness stems from a flaw in their character, whereas our own misbehavior is a momentary glitch in our perfect track record. That person is ick, while we're just having a bad moment on a bad day! But can you prove that that guy who cut you off in traffic *isn't* rushing his pregnant chihuahua to the vet? No. Can you prove that he isn't a demon spawn sent to get on your VERY LAST NERVE? Also no. You might as well assume he did that rude thing for good reasons of his own.

TRY THIS

- When you find yourself internally grumbling about how someone is annoying and dumb
- If you notice that you pretty much always assume other people have bad intentions
- Because life is easier if you're not mad all the time

HOW

1. Do the trickiest thing of all: pay attention to your own inner workings.
2. During times of conflict or tension (inside your head or out in the world), notice if you tend to assume the other person is doing X because they are bad/selfish/greedy/nasty/evil/stinky.
3. If so, pause and remind yourself that you can never get inside someone else's head, and that they probably have a reason for doing X, though you may never know what it is.
4. When appropriate, get curious. Calmly ask them what's going on. That alone can be enough to stop someone in their tracks.
5. BIG BUT: If someone is habitually mean to you, it doesn't matter why. What matters is keeping yourself safe.

UNHELPFUL ADVICE

THERE'S NO TIME LIKE THE PRESENT.

Sure. But maybe a week after never would be even better?

MAY ALL BEINGS EVERYWHERE BE HAPPY AND FREE

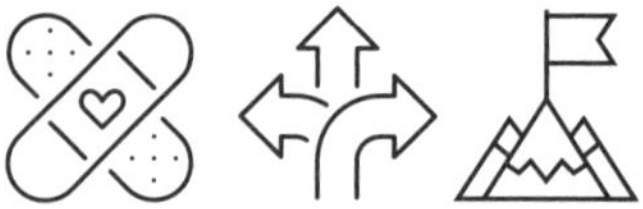

WHY SHOULD I?

Even if the word *mantra* makes you want to puke, there is something mysterious that happens when you repeat reaffirming words. Adapted from the ancient Indian language of Sanskrit, this peace mantra has been recited for thousands of years by people just like you—people who are stressed and want to cultivate loving-kindness as a coping strategy. (Whatever fancy-schmancy jargon people put on things, it pretty much always comes down to that: coping.) Not just for themselves, but for everyone, including frenemies and enemies. Because hurt people hurt people, whereas no one who felt peaceful and loving ever started a social media feud. We could all use a little love, right?

CHEAP THRILL

GO FOREST BATHING.

No, not running through the woods au naturel. Just sit (fully clothed) in a natural space and breathe in. Better, right?

TRY THIS

- When you're caught in feelings of hatred and (unproductive) anger
- Because compassion looks good on you
- When you want to be the change you want to see in the world or whatever

HOW

1. Sit comfortably and close your eyes.
2. Take a few deep breaths.
3. Recite the phrase "May all beings everywhere be happy and free." You can say it out loud, or you can say it internally and coordinate it with your breath, mentally reciting it once on the inhale and once on the exhale. Or simply mentally recite it.
4. Don't puke.
5. Every time you catch your mind wandering, bring it back to the phrase "May all beings everywhere be happy and free."
6. Repeat for one minute or more.
7. Open your eyes and notice how you feel.

Investigate

. . . or Stress-Relief Tactics
That Force You to Look
Down into the Terrifying Abyss
That Is Your Very Soul
Without Flinching

As the saying goes, you're only as sick as your secrets. That includes the secrets of self-deception and a lack of self-awareness. It's simple, really: if your house is flooding, trying to soak up the water with an old mop isn't going to cut it, buddy—you've got to find the broken pipe and deal with the issue at its source. In this stellar metaphor, your mysterious inner workers are the house, the pipe, the flooding water, and the old mop.

WHY INVESTIGATE?

1. **Think of it as cryptozoology.** But instead of chasing Bigfoot or Mothman, you're chasing yourself. You are a strange, strange creature, after all.

2. **Yeah, ignorance is bliss sometimes.** But being ignorant ain't cute.

3. **Once you know, you have options.** Until then, you're basically a preprogrammed robot.

IN-THE-MOMENT JOURNALING

WHY SHOULD I?

When stress is making you uncomfortable, it's fine to deal with it directly. But this strategy falls short when (a) the same discomfort pops up again and again and (b) we skip the part where we figure out what's actually happening. Time for some more inner work, dahlink!

TRY THIS

- When you don't feel like talking
- When your brain feels like a thousand-piece puzzle that's been put in the box and shaken a bunch of times
- When you want to understand your particular brand of weirdness
- When you want to procrastinate doing homework but need to look like you're doing homework

HOW

1. Find a journal that is small enough to fit in your pocket or bag, or use a note-taking app on your phone.
2. When you notice that you're stressed, stop what you're doing.
3. Get out your journal or open the note-taking app. (If the latter, then turn on Do Not Disturb on your phone so you won't be interrupted.)
4. Write down what you notice. You can freewrite, or use the following prompts:
    - Where do you feel the stress in your body? What are the sensations?
    - What kinds of thoughts are you having?
    - What emotions are you feeling?
    - How did you behave? If you didn't *do* anything, what behavioral impulses did you have?
5. Review what you wrote and think about what caused you to feel stressed. How can you alleviate the symptoms or the stress?
6. Think about other times you've noticed the same feelings, so you can get ahead of the stress.

BODY SCAN

WHY SHOULD I?

No, a body scan doesn't require some X-ray tech from a sketchy science lab. All you need to do a body scan—and to stop reactivity in its tracks—is slow down and check in by focusing your attention on each part of your body, noticing sensations as you go. You just notice, then move on, without attempting to change anything. No fixing—got it? Weirdly, your intentional non-effort can inspire relaxation.

TRY THIS

- If you're curious about what's happening internally
- Because you don't want to do something dumb and get hauled off to jail
- To practice noticing and letting go

HOW

1. Get into a comfortable sitting position or lie down on your back. Close your eyes.
2. Begin scanning your body by concentrating on each part. Focus your attention on your toes. What do you feel there? Notice any sensations, like warmth or cold, pain, ease, tightness, tingling, bugs crawling on you, gremlins tickling you, or gravity holding you down. If you're sitting, notice where your toes touch the floor and what that feels like.
3. If you find your focus wandering or thoughts interrupt your scan, notice what's happening and then gently bring your attention back to the physical sensations in your body.
4. Move your attention to your feet, ankles, shins, calves, knees. What sensations do you feel?
5. Move your attention up to your thighs, hips, tuchus, lower back, upper back, neck. What sensations do you find here?
6. Rotate your attention to your belly and chest. What sensations do you find here?
7. Move your attention down your arms, to your elbows and wrists, your hands, fingers, and fingertips.
8. Finally, scan your head, focusing your attention on your face first, then your jaws, ears, forehead, and crown. What sensations do you find here?
9. Take a few moments to reflect on the sensations you noticed throughout your body.
10. Open your eyes.
11. Go get a snack. All this body scanning made you hungry.

GRATITUDE LIST

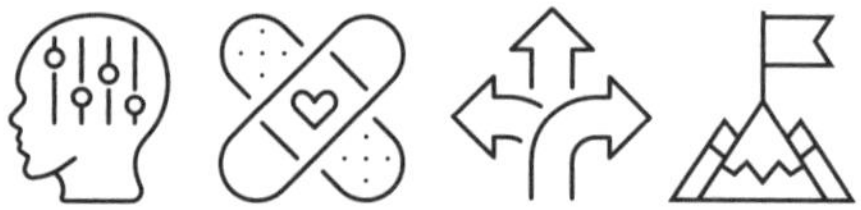

WHY SHOULD I?

Practicing gratitude is about finding the sparkling diamond within the dumpster fire. That broken leg bumming you out? Well, at least you get to spend more time with your ferret. That fight with your dad making you tense? Well, at least chocolate chip cookies exist, and you even have some in your pantry. That F+ on the pop quiz giving you a headache? Well, at least you have a vanilla-scented candle and a grandmother who adores you. See how that works? You don't have to dismiss or ignore the challenges in your life, just take a break from them and pivot toward the sparkle.

An attitude of gratitude improves mood, dude. Sorry about those rhymes—it was unavoidable. Anyway, no matter how sucky life is, it could always be worse. That's meant to be encouraging! Really, practicing gratitude has been linked to improved immunity, sleep, mood, toenail growth, and whistling ability.

TRY THIS

- When you've thrown yourself a pity party
- When your negativity bias is flaring up
- When you've caught yourself comparing
- When you need a reminder that maybe-probably-hopefully things aren't as bad as they might seem

HOW

1. If you still need instructions for how to write, then I don't know what to tell you.
2. Set a timer or make a number goal, or both. For example: *I will write down things I am grateful for for five minutes or until I have twenty items on my list, whichever comes first.*
3. Do it once, do it often. Practicing daily gratitude never hurt anybody.

INTERVIEW

WHY SHOULD I?

Stress can be like a black hole, pulling you into a lightless core from which nothing escapes. Getting someone else's point of view is like boarding a spaceship going turbo-warp-speed or whatever to avoid getting sucked in. Other people might just have interesting stress-escape strategies worth trying. You won't know until you ask!

BUSTED!

STRESS MYTHS DEBUNKED

"Stress comes from ruminating on the past or worrying about the future."

Well, that's a human brain for you.

Also? Sometimes the now can be pretty stressful too.

TRY THIS

- When you (mistakenly) think you are the only one who feels the way you do
- Because talking to other people is generally a good idea

HOW

1. Make a list of people you admire, who seem to have a handle on life, or are really good-looking.
2. Write out a list of questions you'd like to ask them. For example:
    - What do you wish you had known when you were my age?
    - What in your life are you most proud of?
    - Tell me about a time you failed. What did it feel like in the moment? How do you view it now in retrospect?
    - What do you do when you're feeling stressed or overwhelmed?
3. Reach out to your people. Tell them why you admire them, and ask if you could have fifteen minutes of their time. (If it feels scary, do it anyway! The worst that can happen is they don't reply or say no, and so what if they do?)
4. Set up a time to talk.
5. Ask them your questions, being mindful of their time. Take notes or record the interview with their permission.
6. Afterward, write them a thank-you note. It's a pain, but it's the right thing to do.

Organize

. . . or Stress-Relief Tactics
That Let Type A's
Do Their Type-Aing

Ever heard of Occam's razor? It basically means that sometimes the simplest solution is the right one. (Uhhhh, duh?) If you're feeling overwhelmed by a long-term goal or a complicated project, a simple solution is to break it down into milestones that are easy to recognize when you complete them. This has the bonus of giving you a sense of accomplishment, which in turn motivates you to continue working toward your goal.

A FUN NOTE ON GOALS

Goals are good, great, grand, wonderful. But also? Sometimes they're terrible, especially if you haven't fully examined them. The expectations put on you by family, the cultural pressures that shape how you view yourself and your world—these tend to inspire your goals, especially when you're young. And yeah, you do have to fulfill certain requirements that may or may not be exactly your cup of tea, like taking standardized tests or eating broccoli instead of cotton candy. (You will always have to do things you don't want to do. Sorry not sorry: it's just the facts.) Taking a closer look, however, might help you figure out what actually matters to *you*. Ask yourself the following questions, adjusting the goals as you see fit:

- **Do I actually want to** go to Harvard followed by Stanford School of Medicine, become an ophthalmologist, and buy a three-thousand-square-foot house in the suburbs, or is that my parents' goal for me?
- **Do I actually want to** have six-pack abs and buns of absolute steel, or is that just something I saw on TV?
- **Do I actually need to** prove my worth, or am I inherently worthy of love and belonging, clean water, nourishing food, medical care, and a safe place to live?

MANAGEABLE MILESTONES

WHY SHOULD I?

Let's say you have a closet. And into that closet you've been throwing junk that you don't want to deal with for, like, years. Now it's full of junk upon junk upon junk, and you have two weeks to clean it out OR ELSE. That's fourteen days to get it done, including rest days. (Rest days are very important for recovery from hard work—don't forget to schedule them in!) Here is an example of how you might organize your manageable milestones:

Day 1: Look at the mess. Just look at it. Stop avoiding. Feel your feelings.
Day 2: Come up with a strategy (e.g., Every day, I will remove and sort ten items into three piles: trash, donate, and keep.
Day 3: Remove ten items and sort them. When finished, do something to acknowledge this incredible accomplishment, like checking off a checkbox.
Days 4–6: Samesies.
Day 7: Rest.
Day 8: Reassess. Is this strategy working? Will it get you to your goal by Day 14, or do you need to step it up?
Days 9–11: Keep going.
Day 12: Reassess. You're getting close. Are you going to make it?
Day 13: Keep going.
Day 14: FINISH OR ELSE. Then give yourself a treat. You deserve it.

TRY THIS

- When you feel the Procrastination Monster sneaking up on you
- When you are so overwhelmed you feel like quitting before you even begin
- Because you love checking off checklists

HOW

1. Break down the project into a step-by-step list. The more detailed, the better.
2. Count up the number of days until the deadline, or make your own deadline.
3. Assign days to tasks. Include Rest Days. If you think you can accomplish more than one task in a day, then assign multiple tasks to the same day.
4. Reassess and revise as necessary.
5. Track your milestones as you work on your project.
6. Remember: Life happens. Don't be too hard on yourself if you stray from the schedule, unless that motivates you. Then be really hard on yourself! Either way, revise to accommodate the delay.
7. Check off tasks as you complete them, reveling in the sweet, sweet glory of each accomplished milestone. Like, really feel it. It feels so good!
8. Get 'er done.

MAKE A NIGHTLY TO-DO LIST

WHY SHOULD I?

Do you lie in bed at night, thoughts of tomorrow's obligations buzzing like gnats in your head? Some people swear by making nightly to-do lists as part of their wind-down routine. You wash your face, brush your teeth, put on your lacy high-collared Victorian nightclothes, and make a list of all that you have to do the next day. By getting it out of your head and onto paper, you can let it go.

TRY THIS

- When your inner Bossy Boss won't shut up
- Because there is no end to work—but worrying about it when you're trying to sleep isn't exactly productive
- When part of the issue is that you're worried you'll forget something if you don't remind yourself a million times

HOW

1. Put a pad of paper and a pen or pencil by your bed. Not your phone! Devices are not conducive to good sleep hygiene! Put your phone far away!
2. Once you're mostly ready for bed, write down any and all tasks you need to accomplish the next day. They could be related to school, homework, chores, exercise, social engagements, self-care, friends, whatever.
3. Give yourself permission to set down your to-do list. It's not going anywhere—it just exists on that paper over there now, outside your head.
4. Sleep like a log.
5. Repeat nightly.

CHEAP THRILL

CHILLY OUT.

Turn the cold water in your shower all the way up or press an ice pack to your chest. Nothing stops the mental chatter faster than a freeze blast.

DO SOMETHING

WHY SHOULD I?

Our world is a contradiction—as in, it is a miraculous blue-green oasis that supports all of life as we know it, and it's basically a teeming trash heap spinning through a relentless and uncaring void. You, as a singular entity, can decide which Earth you want to live on, and do your teeny-tiny part to make it better (or worse, I guess, if you're into trash heaps).

If the environment isn't your thing, there are plenty of realms, like lots and lots of realms, that could use your help. Volunteer at a food bank or animal shelter, tutor little kids, go canvasing, organize bake sales for a cause you believe in, clean out your closet and donate everything in it. Just *do something!*

TRY THIS

- When you're feeling helpless
- When you feel like the world is ending
- Because litter, overconsumption, and humanity in general is kinda gross

HOW

- Grab a trash bag and go pick up some litter in a park or around your neighborhood. As previously mentioned, litter is gross, so you should probably wear gloves and closed-toe shoes, or use one of those cool mechanical grabber-arm thingies.
- Plant a garden. This can be in your yard, in a community garden, or in a pot on your windowsill.
- Compost. You can get a fancy compost bin, or just put food waste in a bowl on your counter, then dump it at the end of every day in a far corner of your yard and watch what happens (make friends with the local raccoons and squirrels, spy on rats, etc.).
- Get a birdbath to keep those chirpy pollinators hydrated. Doesn't have to be some fancy fountain with a frolicking cherub spitting water into a pool surrounded by gnomes and wind chimes, but it certainly can be.
- Study clean energy and eventually invent a technology that saves the planet. THANK YOU VERY MUCH!

UNHELPFUL ADVICE

~~THE BEST THINGS IN LIFE ARE FREE.~~

Funny thing is, the worst things in life are also free.

Rest

. . . or Stress-Relief Tactics That Involve Blankies, Jammies, and a Stubborn Insistence on Self-Determination in a Hamster-Wheel World

We, as a grind culture, are obsessed with productivity. That's fine. It's just a fact that you have to work hard if you want to compete in this totally weird game we call society. It's all about the bootstraps, babe! The problem arises when we focus only on the grind, the wringing out of every last drop of energy to meet deadlines and line up socks perfectly in the sock drawer. Burnout, decision fatigue, a weakened immune system—all those blahs of chronic stress are a sign that it's high time you sought balance.

WHY GRIND CULTURE IS PROBLEMATIC

1. **It presupposes that hard work leads directly to reward.** Not true, dere. Some of the hardest, most labor- and time-intensive jobs in the world are the least financially compensated. Don't believe me? Ask a teacher.

2. **Marginalized groups are often expected to take on more work for less pay, or to do extra work without compensation.** Case in point: all that uproar about "quiet quitting," a.k.a. younger people doing *just* their jobs instead of chaining themselves to their desks and working around the clock just because. Puh-leaze.

3. **The starting line is all over the map.** Some people have to hustle to pay off the interest on their student loans, while someone else's dad gives them $1M to get their start-up off the ground. Yeah, the second person still has to grind, but they are starting miles ahead.

TAKE A NAP

WHY SHOULD I?

Rumor has it that self-care doesn't always require a purchase. Napping, for one, is free. (Unless you want to buy some kind of smart sleep-pod mattress device for $4,000. You do you, I guess.) And it gets the job done, rest-wise.

TRY THIS

- When you are so tired, you can't see straight
- Because no one but you owns your life/time/energy/body
- When doing stuff seems to only make things worse

HOW

1. Turn off alerts. While you're at it, turn off your phone. And put it in a box. And put that box in another box. And put the box-within-a-box in a room far away.
2. Make your space a haven of coziness. Gather your favorite blankie, your best pillow, your comfiest jammies.
3. Turn on some relaxing music if you're into that.
4. Pull down the blinds or put on a sleeping mask.
5. Call your iguana to join you and snuggle up.
6. Lie down.
7. Close your eyes.
8. Go to sleep already.

UNHELPFUL ADVICE

~~KEEP YOUR NOSE TO THE GRIND-STONE.~~

What even *is* a grindstone? That sounds like it hurts!

YOUR HAPPY PLACE

WHY SHOULD I?

Even in the worst of times, there exists inside you peace and joy, like a cute little mushroom waiting to sprout. That little mushroom is your happy place, which could be an actual place you remember from real life or a fake place you make up for your own mental health. Either way, it's a VIP room, and you are the only VIP.

TRY THIS

- To momentarily escape a crappy reality
- When joy and peace seem as far away as Uranus
- Because mushrooms taste good when sautéed in butter

HOW

1. Sit or lie down. Close your eyes.
2. Take a few deep breaths.
3. Recall or imagine a place where you felt or feel happy. It could be anywhere, anything—a tropical beach you've seen only in pictures, a booth at your favorite diner, snuggled close to a loved one, on the peak of a hike near your house.
4. Imagine yourself there, sitting or swimming or eating a sandwich. It doesn't matter what you're doing, just that you are content within while doing it. Keep it simple, or create an entire movie in your mind.
5. Breathe, imagine, get happy.

UNHELPFUL ADVICE

JUST CLEAR YOUR MIND.

Nope, a mind is not a hard drive. That's not gonna happen.

LIGHT AS A FEATHER, HEAVY AS A SANDBAG

WHY SHOULD I?

There's an ancient practice called yoga nidra, or yogic sleep. No Chaturangas or Warrior IIs involved—instead, you use your mind to calm yourself. Not by shouting in your head, *Calm down, you knotted yarn-ball of nerves!* That doesn't really work, though you are welcome to try. Rather, you let your body fully rest while mentally doing some simple practices, like focusing on your breath, scanning your body, using visualization, or witnessing your thoughts.

TRY THIS

- When you have physical aches or pains
- When you want to experience the awesome power of your mind
- When you need an excuse to lie down

HOW

1. Find a quiet place to lie down, preferably somewhere other than your bed. We all know that if you lie down in your bed, you will fall asleep. If the floor is covered in dirty clothes and discarded shoes, then clean it up, you slob!
2. Fidget and wiggle until you find a comfortable position.
3. Close your eyes.
4. Mentally follow the course of your breath, in and out through the nose (unless you're stuffed up, then go ahead and be a mouth breather). Follow the inhale into your lungs, noticing the rise and then fall of your chest with the exhale. If your abs are clenching, unclench them.
5. Try not to fall asleep.
6. Scan your body, each part at a time, from your toes to the top of your head. No need to do anything about any sensations you find—simply notice them and move on.
7. Become aware of your entire body as a whole. Not easy, is it?
8. Try not to fall asleep.
9. Now let your body be heavy, as though you are filled with sand, and imagine the floor beneath you is soft, like you could sink down into it.
10. Be heavy.
11. Now let your body be light, as though you are filled with air, as light as a feather. Imagine your body floating up toward the ceiling.
12. Be light.
13. Try not to fall asleep.
14. Go back and forth a few times between heavy and light.
15. Let go of this practice and return to your breath.
16. Are you asleep? Wake up.

Breathe

. . . or Stress-Relief Tactics That Involve Controlling This Thing That Your Body Does Automatically

People really love breathing. That's because you have to do it or else you die. Also, the practice of controlled breathing is like giving a little nudge to your parasympathetic nervous system. It can help lower your blood pressure, slow your heartbeat, get more oxygen to your brain, and—you guessed it—calm you down.

When you're in fight or flight (or freeze or fawn), however, it's easy to forget this simple tool. In fact, pausing to take a few big breaths might be the last thing that occurs to you. That's why it's helpful to practice breathing when you aren't in panic mode. This will not only make it so you won't have to think too hard about each step, but it'll also help you experience breathing's effects. And when a stressful situation arises, you'll be more likely to remember that this little thing called breathing actually works.

WHY BREATHING IS NEAT

1. **It's free.**
2. **It's essential.**
3. **It's effective for improving all kinds of life-related things. Really, it is!**
4. **It's mandatory.**

BASIC BELLY BREATHING

WHY SHOULD I?

When we get stressed, we tend to take shallow, quick breaths. When we are relaxed or asleep, we naturally breathe more slowly and deeply. Belly breathing, a.k.a. abdominal or diaphragmatic breathing, is a fake-it-till-you-make-it practice—you might not feel relaxed, but if you consciously breathe as though you are, you might just get there.

TRY THIS

- When you notice you're breathing shallowly
- When you're hyped up like a hummingbird
- When you've got a presentation or some other event that's making you nervous
- Anytime

HOW

1. Set a timer for five minutes.
2. Sit up straight on a block on the floor or in a chair, or lie down on your back in a comfortable position.
3. Put your hands on your belly.
4. Breathe in slowly and deeply through your nose, allowing your belly to expand. Notice strain elsewhere in the body and try to let it go. Let your belly do the work.
5. Exhale softly and slowly through your lips, as if you were blowing on a spoonful of hot soup, until your lungs are empty. Pull your belly button toward your spine.
6. Repeat, and notice how you just chillllllll out.

BUSTED!

STRESS MYTHS DEBUNKED

"Self-care is the cure for stress."

If only we could just bubble-bath our way out of stress . . .

Self-care is great, but life will still be there once the water has cooled and the chill-out playlist has run its course. Hopefully you'll be better able to deal, however, once you've toweled off.

HEART/BELLY BREATHING

WHY SHOULD I?

You literally breathe when your diaphragm contracts to pull downward and the muscles over your ribs and sternum pull upward, creating a kind of vacuum that draws yummy oxygen into the lungs. You metaphorically breathe into your heart and belly, your stomach rising on the inhale and softening down on the exhale. This natural motion can be calming, which leads to calmer breathing, which leads to feeling calmer, and so on.

TRY THIS

- When you just need a freaking minute
- Because the best self-care practices don't cost a thing

HOW

1. Lie down on your back.
2. Put one hand on your chest, one hand on your belly.
3. Close your eyes.
4. Inhaling slowly and deeply, imagine that you are breathing into your hands.
5. Exhale slowly, noticing your chest and belly sinking down.
6. Repeat for ten breaths or longer.
7. Before you get up, take time to reflect. How do you feel now?

UNHELPFUL ADVICE

JUST RELAX

Wow, why didn't I think of that?
Of *course* it's just that simple.

BOX BREATHING

WHY SHOULD I?

Box breathing, a.k.a. square breathing, is another relaxation technique. It requires the ability to count to four, however, so if that's a problem for you, go ahead and skip this one.

TRY THIS

- When you're feeling panicky
- If you have two minutes to calm down before some big event

HOW

1. Set a timer for two to five minutes. Or set a focus goal of a number of box breaths to complete (e.g., ten boxes).
2. Breathe in through your nose as you count to four. Imagine your breath is drawing the top of a square.
3. Hold your breath as you count to four. Imagine drawing the right side of a box as you count.
4. Breathe out as you count to four. Imagine drawing the bottom of a square as you count.

5. Hold your lungs empty as you count to four. Imagine drawing the left side of a box as you count.
6. Repeat until the timer goes off, or you reach your box breathing goal.
7. Pause. Note how you feel in your body/mind. Do you feel the same as you did before you started the box breathing, or do you feel different?

BUSTED!

STRESS MYTHS DEBUNKED

"Stress causes cancer."

While stress does impact our bodies and make us more susceptible to certain ailments, there is no direct correlation between cancer and stress. *And thinking that being stressed gives you cancer is only going to stress you out!*

Move

. . . or Stress-Relief Tactics
That Involve Activating
the Skin Bag Full of Bones
and Guts and Stuff
That Is You

As previously noted, you have a body. It's a very needy thing, requiring an abundance of upkeep: feeding, watering, sunlighting, sleeping, hairstyling, nail filing, butt and teeth cleaning (not with the same instrument). And it needs exercise!

If you believe scientists, then exercise does everything. It improves mood and boosts energy. It promotes better sleep and cognitive function. It can help prevent or manage blood pressure, mood disorders, arthritis, cardiovascular disease, even cancer. It's fun, or at least fun-adjacent!

DISCLAIMER

If you are brand-spanking-new to moving, the following exercises are unfamiliar to you, or they are not accessible for whatever reason, ask a PE teacher, coach, or someone sporty in your life who knows what they're talking about for assistance. Adapt the movements for yourself, and lower (or raise) the intensity or movement to make it safe (and fun?) for you.

EXERCISES DEFINITELY WORTH TRYING

- Dog walking
- Punk rock aerobics
- Circus class
- Dance partying
- Live action role-playing (wearing chain mail is excellent weight training)
- Aqua aerobics
- "Active meetings" with friends (a.k.a. go for a walk)
- Handstands
- Tag, Capture the Flag, or Red Rover
- Paddleboarding
- The Floor Is Lava!
- Piggybacking
- Pogo sticking
- Singing karaoke (with passion)
- Jazz hands
- Rollerblading (skintight neon bodysuit optional)
- Professional axe throwing
- Trampolining

SYNC MOVEMENT AND BREATH

WHY SHOULD I?

Vinyasa means "to place in a special way" and is often used to describe the yoga practice of coordinating movement and breath in a flowing sequence. But yoga doesn't have this on lock; many practices have this kind of coordination, like martial arts, weight lifting, swimming, and so on. As the ancient sages once said, "Get swole, brah."

TRY THIS

- If you're too restless or agitated to sit still to meditate or do breathing practices
- When you want to improve in your sport
- Because your body starts to feel like stale peanut brittle if you don't move it enough

HOW

You can coordinate breath with any movement. Try the following exercise to get you started; it can be done standing or sitting.

1. Inhale and exhale three times to center your focus.
2. With arms by your sides, inhale and turn your face to the right.
3. Exhale and face forward.
4. Inhale and turn your face to the left.
5. Exhale and face forward.
6. Repeat three times.
7. Inhale while raising your arms above your head.
8. Exhale while lowering your arms to your sides.
9. Repeat three times.
10. Add movement as desired, coordinating one movement per inhale, one movement per exhale.

UNHELPFUL ADVICE

~~JUST TAKE THINGS ONE DAY AT A TIME.~~

As opposed to what?

INTENSE EXERCISE

WHY SHOULD I?

Short bursts of high-intensity cardio that get your heart thumping make it so you pretty much can't think about anything but how hard you're working. Then the resting intervals give you time to catch your breath and reflect on the ouchiness of the aforementioned cardio. Is it a form of torture? Jury's out. Regardless, it moves stuck energy and gives you all the sweet health benefits of exercise.

TRY THIS

- When you feel like punching the wall or doing something equally destructive
- When you want to push yourself out of a rut
- Because exercise is one of the few things that is almost always good for you

HOW

1. Get an old-fashioned clock with an actual second hand or an old-fashioned timer. Or open the timer app on your phone. If you want to get real fancy, download a HIIT (high-intensity interval training) app.
2. Start with the goal of thirty seconds on, thirty seconds off, for five minutes.

CHEAP THRILL

DO 100 PUSH-UPS.

Or as many as you can do, stopping short of barfing and/or breaking yourself. Not thinking about your little problems now, are you?

3. Choose up to five high-intensity cardio exercises. These could be running, jumping jacks, burpees, jumping rope, high knee jumps, push-ups, lunges, pull-ups, squats, et cetera. Really, there are a million exercises out there. Do your chosen exercise as fast as you can without sacrificing form (i.e., maintaining good alignment to keep yourself safe).
4. Set your timer/clock/app and go: thirty seconds doing your cardio exercise, thirty seconds resting or light stretching. Do this for five minutes. That's a total of five high-intensity moments and five recovery moments.
5. At the end, before you skip off to grab a drink of water and a shower, note how you feel.
6. Do it again the next day. Add more time and change up exercises as desired.
7. Get super ripped.

STROLL

WHY SHOULD I?

A change of scenery plus a simple, no-tech activity can go a long way toward stress reduction. That's why there are a whole bunch of cheesy quotes from famous philosophers, writers, artists, and entrepreneurs about walking. Give it a try, or put a spin on it by tracking steps, forest bathing (it's a thing), or practicing mindfulness movement while you're at it.

TRY THIS

- When you want to move but don't need any bells or whistles
- When screens are making your eyeballs feel like cotton balls
- If you have a dog or are taking care of a baby in need of a snooze cruise

HOW

1. Brush your teeth, put on some clothes, and run a comb through your hair, for goodness' sake!
2. Go outside.
3. Walk.

- Add-on: Tracking steps. Track your steps with whatever device you use, but don't look until you're done meandering. How many steps did it take you to lose yourself?

- Add-on: Forest bathing. Take this whole activity to somewhere with a bunch of trees. Revel in the soothing greenness, the scent of leaves, the breeze, and so on. (Can also be done in alternative natural environments, like on a beach or mountainside.)
- Add-on: Moving mindfulness. Focus on walking; your breath; the sensation of your muscles relaxing and contracting with every step; the feeling of your feet on the ground; the sights, smells, and sounds around you. Every time a thought pops up, notice it, then let it go and bring your attention back to your walking.

BUSTED!

STRESS MYTHS DEBUNKED

"Avoiding triggers will keep you from being stressed."

That'll work great! If you live in a magical paradise where every single one of your needs is immediately attended to without you having to ask, that is. *For the rest of us who live in the real world, there will always be triggers to manage.*

Laugh

. . . or Stress-Relief Tactics That Are Basically You Goofing Off

Yay, it's everyone's favorite stress buster! That's because not only is laughing fun, but it's super-duper good for you, according to Science. On a physical level, it makes you breathe, it lowers your blood pressure, and it gives some key muscles a workout. Apparently, it also improves your immune system and relieves pain too! On a mental level, laughing takes your mind off whatever thingy you've been worrying about, plus the very nature of comedy is that it takes hard things—like a miscommunication or an awkward interaction or being a lonely cat person—and puts a humorous spin on them. Emotionally: well, sadness and pain don't hurt so much when you're giggling. Let's not forget behavioral stress: when you're laughing, you are probably not doing problematic activities like running your homework through a shredder.

4

HILARIOUS JOKES TO GET YOU STARTED:

What's the difference between apathy and ignorance?
Don't know, don't care.

Why did the skeleton skip the prom?
Because he had no body to go with.

Why should you never criticize someone until you've walked a mile in their shoes?
That way, when you criticize them, you'll be a mile away, and you'll have their shoes.

What's the best way to use a stress ball?
Throw it at the last person who annoyed you.

WATCH COMEDY

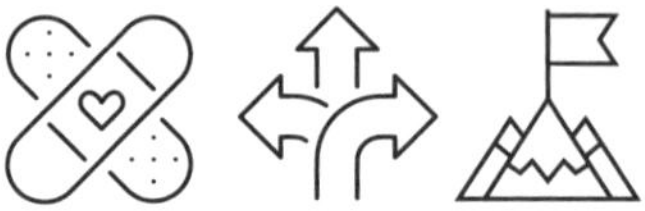

WHY SHOULD I?

Pop some popcorn, put your feet up, and turn on your favorite sitcom, sketch show, funny movie, or stand-up comedy act. That's it.

TRY THIS

- When you want a reason to watch TV
- When you're sick in bed
- When everything seems super-duper serious

HOW

1. Turn on the TV.
2. Find something funny to watch.
3. Watch it.
4. Laugh.

UNHELPFUL ADVICE

~~JUST POWER THROUGH.~~

Sure, but what if the ole tank is completely empty?

UNHELPFUL ADVICE

YOUTH IS WASTED ON THE YOUNG.

And I'm supposed to do what with that, exactly?

FORCE LAUGHTER

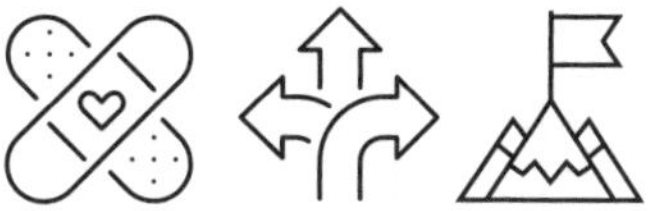

WHY SHOULD I?

Laughter of any kind is good medicine. This practice has the added benefit of forcing you not just to get over it but to get over *yourself*, because initially you will look and feel like an idiot. You need at least one other person for this little game, and they need to be willing to look and feel like an idiot too. When trying to convince someone to look like an idiot with you, phrase it this way: "If you really like/love/care about me, then you will do this truly ridiculous but harmless activity with me." Guilt works!

TRY THIS

- When you are taking yourself too seriously
- When you want to practice being embarrassed
- When you're sick of crying

HOW

1. You and whoever you've wrangled start laughing. This is probably going to be fake, as in you saying, "Ha ha ha, ho ho ho, he he he."
2. Be embarrassed.
3. Keep going.
4. Wonder why you're doing this and if you should stop.
5. Keep going some more, until you start laughing for real.
6. Laugh some more.

Unplug

. . . or Stress-Relief Tactics That Might Make You Feel Like You Are Missing the Most Important Part of Yourself, Which Is the Whole Freaking Point

Once upon a time—a long, long, long time ago—phones were attached to walls. Computers were the size of garages, and no one but scientists had them anyway. Televisions were as blocky as suitcases, and there were only a few channels operating for a few hours every day. Mail was letters written in cursive, letters that took days and weeks to send and receive. Cameras were just cameras. Newspapers arrived on your doorstep, in the form of paper and smelly ink. Maps, too, took the form of paper and ink, with zero narration. Nothing was "smart." Nothing!

In those olden days of yore, you would leave the house and no one could reach you, find you, or send you pictures of their cat or their donut/spaghetti/pizza. If you got lost, you asked a real-live human for directions. If you got bored, you . . . were bored. It was magical! It was terrible!

NOW YOU TRY.

PERSONAL RECORD SCROLLING LIMIT

WHY SHOULD I?

It's so easy to get caught in a scroll only to look up and realize three hours have gone by. Where did they go? The same place where all your hair ties and single missing socks have gone. What do you have to show for it? Mush brain and the beginning of a hunch in your back. If you find yourself losing time in this fashion, it would behoove you to start rolling back the scrolling. That time would be much better spent doing . . . anything else.

TRY THIS

- When you frequently feel rushed yet somehow regularly manage to lose yourself in your phone
- When you start developing a minor case of carpal tunnel syndrome
- When you stop being able to tell the difference between virtual reality and reality reality

HOW

1. Track how long you use your phone or device every day. Some devices have "Screen Time" stats in Settings, where you can find your daily average over the course of a week.
2. Note which apps you use the most, between social media, messaging, games, shopping, education, entertainment, news, cooking, tools, et cetera. Of these, which have a positive impact on you, and which might be negative?
3. Set a big specific goal, like "I will scroll for a maximum total of forty-five minutes per day."
4. Set smaller incremental goals toward that big goal, like "I will be on my phone for five minutes less today than I was yesterday" or "I will use social media for a max of fifteen minutes per day, shop online for a max of ten minutes, and use entertainment apps for a total of half an hour."
5. Go for your incremental goals, trying to beat your personal record day by day until you reach your big goal.
6. Go explore reality reality. It's kinda neat, huh?

BUSTED!

STRESS MYTHS DEBUNKED

"You can tell if someone is stressed."

Sometimes true, sometimes not.
Stress shows up, or is hidden, differently for everyone.
Maybe you're not stressed—your hair just always looks like that.

DEVICE-FREE DAYS

WHY SHOULD I?

Picture yourself frolicking through a meadow, nothing in your hands, your face tipped toward the great blue sky. Perhaps you are wearing a long flowy dress that swirls around you as you spin, your arms spread wide in delight. Or perhaps your shorts are blowing in the breeze. Is this the best day of your life? Maybe. What's missing from this picture? A device!

TRY THIS

- When social media comparisons feel like a kick to the self-esteem
- When your phone feels like an actual part of your actual body, like a third hand or something
- Because you need to learn to live without a device to prepare for the impending alien invasion/apocalypse/dolphin world domination

HOW

1. Turn off your device.
2. Put it in a dresser drawer.
3. Duct-tape the drawer shut.
4. Throw the whole bureau in the ocean.
5. Leave it there for an hour, working your way up to an entire day.
6. Put on a flowy dress or some shorts and spin, arms spread wide with delight.

UNHELPFUL ADVICE

~~TIME IS MONEY~~

Sounds fake, but OK.

LET IT BE

Well, here we are, at the end of our stress guide journey. If you were hoping for some simple, straightforward info you could tie up in a neat little bow, some quick fixes and hot tips and tricks that would make life easy from here on out . . . sorry. Stress just isn't like that. *Life* isn't like that. All you can do is brush your teeth, wash your face, and carry on. And remember:

- Your experience is normal.
- When one thing doesn't work, you can always try something new.
- The best things in life don't cost $999.99.
- This, too, shall pass.
- You're doing a good job.
- The mess is what makes life interesting.

ARE YOU OVER IT YET?

No? There's only one thing to do: KEEP TRYING FOREVER.